£3·50
L HRB

The Little Book of
Slugs

Edited by
 nd Suzanne Galant

D0414787

© CAT Publications 2002
The Centre for Alternative Technology Charity Ltd.
Machynlleth, Powys, SY20 9AZ, UK
Tel. 01654 705980 Fax. 01654 702782
email: pubs@cat.org.uk Web: www.cat.org.uk
Registered Charity No. 265239.

The right of Allan Shepherd and Suzanne Galant to be identified as the editors of
this work has been asserted by them in accordance with the Copyright,
Designs and Patents Act 1986.

All rights reserved. No part of this publication may be reproduced, stored in a retrieval
system, or transmitted, in any form, or by means, electronic, mechanical, photocopying,
recording or otherwise, without the prior permission of the copyright owner.

ISBN 1 90217 513 1
1 2 3 4 5 6 7 8 9 10

Mail Order copies from: *Buy Green By Mail*, Tel. 01654 705959.
The details are provided in good faith and believed to be correct at
the time of writing, however no responsibility is taken for any errors.
Our publications are updated regularly; please let us know of any
amendments or additions which you think may be useful for future editions.

Printed in Great Britain by Welshpool Printing Group Ltd.
on paper obtained from sustainable sources.

Contents

Don't Be Sluggish

– introducing *The Little Book of Slugs*

To Humphrey Bogart a slug was a bullet in the chest from a .45, but to any gardener the word conjures up trouble of a different kind. Loathe them or like them (and believe it or not there are some doctors of academe who devote a large part of their lives to studying them), the slug is the kind of trouble you just can't ignore. As Humph' might have said, doing nothing is not an option.

The chemical slug pellet

But what *do* you do about public enemy number one? Most people (85 per cent according to one poll) choose to deliver a blue bullet in the shape of the chemical slug pellet – 400 billion are sprinkled every year on British gardens alone. But out of the 85 per cent who do use slug pellets only 32 per cent really want to. The remaining 53 per cent use them reluctantly or as a second choice if the first fails. Given an effective alternative most people would use something else.

So why are people reluctant to use slug pellets? According to manufacturers the 15 per cent who never use slug pellets don't use them because they think they are a threat to wildlife. We don't know whether this broad definition includes pets.

Most manufacturers are in two minds about the dangers of their own product. Although they warn the consumer that their product can be hazardous to pets and children, they also claim that it is only dangerous when incorrectly used. They say that their critics never produce any figures when they criticize their product, and report untruths that build unnecessary fear in consumers.

The pro- and anti-pellet battle lines are drawn along stereotypical lines: in the blue corner, are the manufacturers and retailers of pesticides; in the green corner are the wildlife and environmental organisations, the producers of organic and non-chemical alternatives to the slug pellet and animal welfare groups, including the Guide Dogs for the Blind Association (who lost a newly trained dog to slug pellet poisoning in 2002). Between them they make up two giant sets of interest groups slugging it out.

Somewhere in the midst of claim and counter claim are the facts – the dry government reports, the veterinary records and people's stories – although as we discovered, retrieving the facts and putting them together is quite a process.

So here they are:

- Slug pellets are poisoned cereal chunks. Metaldehyde and methiocarb – the two most common slug poisons – would not on their own be an attractive proposition to slugs. Slugs prefer to eat nice young shoots, so manufacturers have to put the poison in a bait, and by law the bait must be more attractive than the plants. Unfortunately, these cereal chunks also attract mammals, birds, and some insects – causing death or injury if consumed in large enough quantities.
  - Manufacturers do take precautions to deter animals and birds but these do not stop some animals eating the pellets.

• Slug pellets do kill and cause distress to animals.
The Government's annual study *Pesticide Poisoning of Animals* shows that animals are poisoned by slug pellets every year. The Veterinary Poisons Information Service (VPIS), an advisory organisation for vets only, keeps records of deaths and illness caused by slug pellet poisoning. In 2001 they recorded ninety six cases of poisoning, including seven fatalities. Visit our website www.ihateslugs.com for more details or send an S.A.E. to Allan Shepherd for our factsheet 'What's Wrong With Slug Pellets?'

• Slug pellets can poison animals even when they have been used properly. The 2000 report on *Pesticide Poisoning of Animals* cites one case of an animal being poisoned after walking along the edge of a field where pellets had been correctly applied.

• Slug pellets can poison pets whether they are eaten from the packet or the garden. The VPIS has records of both cases. The fatalities occur when an animal (usually a dog) eats the pellets direct from the packaging.

• Slug pellets made from methiocarb poison predator beetles.

• Slug pellets kill other predators such as birds and hedgehogs.

• It is impossible to calculate the real threat to the environment because few people report wildlife deaths. The Wildlife Incident Investigation Scheme (WIIS) investigates a few hundred cases every year but most wild animals will go to ground when they are ill and will never be found.

• Slug pellets do not meet organic standards.

So why do people use them?

Slug pellets are convenient, easy to use, effective and cheap, and of course these are the qualities that most consumers respond to – although pet owners may think differently when faced with a trip to the vet and the subsequent bill. So is there any alternative that can match these qualities? The closest commercial product is probably Nemaslug, a culture of nematodes which burrow their way into the slug and ruin its appetite until it eventually dies. Although this is currently more expensive than slug pellets, it is easy to use and does not harm any other living creature.

While some of the solutions work for some they do not work for others, or all of the time. Some, such as beer traps, are hardly sustainable, or organic (unless you're using waste organic beer, of course) and may also drown predator beetles. However, at least now we have a choice. If one method doesn't work, try another, or a combination of approaches. Coming up with solutions to environmental problems should be fun, and what could be more fun than playing in the garden?

Bug-the-Slug

Tough on slime. Tough on the causes of slime.

'I wrote SLUGS! YOU CAN END IT ALL HERE in foot-high salt letters outside my back door. The morning brought a sight of devastation that will never leave me. I wasn't surprised that slugs are tired of life, but frankly gobsmacked that 95 per cent decided to hurl themselves onto the word HERE, which seemed almost Japanese in its effortless combination of suicide and courtesy.'

Hugo Rune was one of the first Bug-the-Slug contributors and one of the most memorable. As we were soon to discover he was not alone with his unsuppressed feelings of desperation.

As the Bug-the-Slug campaign developed we quickly identified an emerging behavioural pattern amongst contributors.

Slug busters were:

obsessional – 'Last night alone I collected 588!!!
And since I started keeping a record on 23rd May I have bagged 2,358.'
Mrs Whately;

dedicated – 'I have collected at least 5 litres of slugs and snails from my 3 metres by 15 metres garden.'
Jo Wainright;

eccentric – 'You can spend hours just watching a slug breathe.'
Chris Madsen.

And at the extremes – well, we'll save those for later.

Interestingly, there was no consistent approach to the question of death. Surprisingly large numbers couldn't kill, instead choosing deterrents, or in some unscrupulous cases the surreptitious yet gentle sport of neighbours' fence pitch-and-toss (mentioning no names). There were, of course, those like Joanna Taylor who hated the thought of killing any living creature but were "thinking of making an exception with slugs." And if we had our share of the good, we definitely had the bad and the ugly. Take this anonymous contributor: "My friend Emily from Amsterdam was visiting friends in Yatton. She said to me of one of them, 'I think Julie is a very cold person; she stabs slugs with a screwdriver.'"

We also had a certain amount of philosophy:

"The most frightening war is a psychological one. Just suppose for a minute that slugs are the stronger side and that their ability to change our human response is a conscious one. After all they seem to encourage us to garden organically, thus increasing their chances of survival and of course enjoying a better diet. Any species that allows you to pick it up and destroy it in so many different ways must have a few tricks up its sleeves. Maybe this non-violent action is a sign of philosophical superiority, perhaps we could learn a few lessons from these slow moving but ruthless warriors.

I have no doubt that they will exist on this planet long after we have gone, so just maybe there are aliens at the bottom of my garden."

Bill Cayless

And if slugs in the garden weren't bad enough spare a thought for Alison Carter, who, on moving into her new house, was introduced to two resident pets: "We bought the old house from a lady who introduced us to the two usual slugs, Pat and Fred. They visited us at night and could be encountered if we came downstairs any time after lights out. I'm always stepping on them." We guess you won't be surprised to discover that slugs can stretch up to 20 times their own length.

So read on and find out how you can deal with the slugs in your life. But before you do, take some time to get to know your enemy – for it might save you a lot of effort in the long run.

Read the first chapter first and discover the Achilles heel of the single footed slug – it could affect the way you deal with them.

Part Two has some of the best contributions from www.ihateslugs.com – our Bug-the-Slug campaign website.

Part Three includes lists of slug resistant plants and full details of what we do at The Centre for Alternative Technology.

So good luck with your slug busting and as CAT's Head Gardener Roger McLennan would say, "don't be sluggish."

Part One

Know Your Enemy: the secret life of the slug

"Personally, I think the gardener needs to understand the slug in order to outwit it."
Diane Oldham

Perhaps at this moment of time this statement makes you feel angry. "Understand them. I just want to kill them." It's hard when you've just lost something dear to you, but you really must chill out and take some time to get to know your enemy. In the long run it may just save your sanity.

Lesson number one:

THE SLUG CANNOT SURVIVE WITHOUT MOISTURE

The slug is just one of 90,000 species of gastropod – but don't worry too much, most of these are in the sea or the Tropics. In fact Britain only has thirty different species of slug and only four of these – the field slug, garden slug, keel slug and black slug – will eat your plants.

The key to understanding the slug is remembering that they came from the sea and can only survive on land because their gills have evolved into lungs. They are still dependent on moisture for survival. They have no form of protective skin and are at constant risk of dehydration as soon as the air humidity drops below 100 per cent.

Having said this, "Britain is the slug capital of the world, nowhere else has such ideal conditions." – Invertebrate Ecologist and slug expert, Dr Bill Symondson

Your response...

You need to watch out for ideal slug conditions – a warm, wet night typically, but also a humid evening or a dew-damp morning. Although slugs will move in the day during excessive wet spells, most venture out at night because they fear loss of humidity. When the conditions are right you need to take action. Picking off is perhaps the most effective response and you can help this process by creating removable hiding places for them. This allows you to maintain some control by having some idea where they might be hanging out. You can also make life harder by keeping your garden free of damp, dark areas – at least in the places where it matters most.

Lesson number two:

SLUGS LOSE WATER THROUGH THEIR SLIME AND HAVE TO KEEP EATING AND DRINKING IF THEY WANT TO KEEP MOVING

If you watch a slug through a pane of glass you will behold a thing of great beauty – the muscular movement of its one giant foot (we found this out by chance when filming for a TV news broadcast). The slug contracts a series of muscles on the underside of its body, creating a wave that moves from the back end to the head. It looked like the kind of ripple of light effect you get from the more sophisticated Christmas fairy lights. The slime trail you see behind a slug comes from the pedal mucus gland. This allows them to move along, but as 98 per cent of it is water, movement dehydrates them.

Your response…

Slugs have to hide and eat in dry conditions and move when it's damp.
If it's hot and dry and you need to water, drip feed plants individually or
water the base of the plants only. If it's damp, remove pit stops along the
route and put up barriers. Slugs have a good memory for nice food so
they will have a regular route – and great determination.

Lesson number three:

SLUGS LIKE CERTAIN PLANTS AT CERTAIN STAGES OF THE GROWTH OF THESE PLANTS

No surprises here – as any gardener who has lost another batch of young radishes knows. At first glance your average slug doesn't look like a creature with a sophisticated palate but in fact it is. The slug favours a varied diet and can judge the quality of food from some distance. The slug will also look out for young shoots, which are rich in water and nutrients.

Your response...

Don't sow direct to ground if you can help it.
Grow seedlings in protected areas (use some of the methods described in this book) using a good sowing compost mix to give them strong early growth. CAT gardener Roger McLennan uses a mix of two parts soil, one part leaf mould and one part sand. If possible raise seedlings off the ground and grow them in a greenhouse or polytunnel. When you plant them out put some distance between your seedlings and the slugs – try and create an exclusion zone, using a combination of careful husbandry, boundaries and nightly slug hunts.

Lesson number four:

SLUGS NEED PERFECT CONDITIONS TO MATE: HUMID, NOT TOO COLD, AND AT NIGHT

Slugs are actually hermaphrodites, which means they contain the reproductive organs of both sexes. However, they are not male and female at the same time. They start off male and produce sperm, which is stored in special pockets. They only become female after sex when they produce ova which they can fertilize themselves.

Your response...

Not much you can do about this one. Unless you are truly obsessive you may as well lie back and think of their amazing courtship, which includes between 30 and 90 minutes of mutual caresses, a mid-air nuptual embrace as they dangle from a twisted cord of thickened mucus and the final glorious exchange of their blue, club-shaped penis sacs.

Voilà

Lesson number five:

SLUGS CAN BE USEFUL

No, it can't be true. I'm afraid so, as anyone who has ever asked the question "what is the point of the slug?" – and let's face it that's probably most of us – is about to find out. The slug uses its radula – with its thousands of tiny tooth-like protrusions – to munch away at decaying vegetable and animal matter. Anyone who walks down a country lane after a rain storm will also note that slugs eat other slugs – although as they are already dead this does not make them any more appealing.

Your response…

As they break down the dead, they are a useful addition to the compost heap. They help to get the process of decomposition started. Adding compost to the soil helps your plants grow stronger which makes them more resistant to the slug. So there you are, the slug helps you to wage war against itself – a neat little virtuous circle.

Top 4 slugs to worry about

"My Dad always called all the slugs and snails 'Oliver's Army'" –
Diane Lock

The field slug

Length – up to 4cm; colour – grey/fawn; mucus – colourless or white;
dining habits – typically found on lettuces and cabbages,
but will eat almost everything.

The garden slug

Length – up to 3cm; colour – blackish with a paler side strip;
dining habits – the stems of young beans and marrow plants, the roots
of turnips and beetroot, the tubers of potatoes.

The keel slug

Length – up to 6cm; colour - dark grey/olive with a yellow or orange stripe along the ridge; dining habits – a specialist burrower notorious for liking a nice bit of potato, in fact most root crops.

The black slug

Length – up to 20cm; colour – surprisingly, white, red, orange or grey are all common, although, of course, black is most usual; dining habits – rarely as destructive as the three smaller species described above but can cause damage in spring. Prefers rotting vegetation as the year wears on. May rock from side to side when disturbed!

Part Two

Slug Busters

Predators

"Hedgehogs are excellent slug destroyers! Encourage them into your garden by building a hedgehog home, or offering food such as meat-based cat or dog food, and always ensure there is a supply of fresh water."
British Hedgehog Preservation Society

"In the Western Isles the Community Council is ridding the islands of their hedgehog population to improve the chances of ground nesting birds. These hedgehogs will be rehomed on the mainland. So offer your services and ask to look after some hedgehogs in your garden."
Jenny Strachan

Top five slug predators

– in no scientifically determined order

5. Birds – especially ducks and chickens.

4. Frogs and toads.

3. Hedgehogs – if you put out pet food, the slugs will eat and be eaten.

2. Arthropods – centipedes, glow worms, ground beetles and even daddy long legs (crane flies).

1. The slow worm – according to some the most efficient predator, partly because they tend to hide out in similar places during the day.

And bubbling under…but not so good for the garden…
moles, shrews, badgers and rats.

You can also buy-in a natural predator, a nematode worm branded Nemaslug. This burrows its way into the slug and makes its home there.

After three days Mr Slug has lost his appetite.

After ten days he is dead.

Leave it to nature

"My bantams play a major role in eating slugs. In the winter they can roam about freely and the minor damage to brassica plants is outweighed by the good they do. The bantams also attract partridges and pheasants who also predate on slugs. I have created a wildlife haven with four small ponds, rampant hedges and borders filled with cottage plants and fruit trees, which in turn attract frogs, toads, newts and many birds. The main path is covered in bark (not slug friendly) and I don't really have any major pest problems."

Jane Page

Hole in the toad

– let them fill up with slugs

"Best of all methods, is frogs and toads. So get a pond and allow wildlife to inhabit it – birds will drink, hedgehogs too. Blackbirds love slugs, so feed the birds your unwanted slimys and help the environment too!"
Katie Bailey

"We rarely see any slugs in our 110 foot city garden and have always assumed it is because of the amount of frogs and toads we have in and around the pond."
Trefor Lloyd

"I now keep a couple of large dappled slugs as pets in an old coal bunker – away from the frogs."
Charlie Hall

Give them the bird

"We have had Indian Runner ducks for two years and have had no
slugs in the garden at all, plus the ducks don't eat young or small plants.
No poisons are used and they produce wonderful fresh eggs.
Khaki Campbells also eat slugs, but Indian Runners are the
best slug deterrents."
Rose and Pete Challands

"I take great care to keep cats out of my garden and to encourage birds.
These are the front-line defenders!! We shouldn't be depriving
them of food."
John Richardson

"I catch slugs and snails by hand in the garden, then put them in a box and take them to some waste ground nearby, where there are lots of thrushes who like to eat them. That way I am also helping the endangered thrush population!"
Emma Hudson

"The most organic way to keep your garden slug and pest free is to keep a few hens – size and number to suit your space."
Anne Hodgson

Not so fast...

Predators really are wonderful things, but spare a thought for the hapless
chicken as it triggers the slug's wonderful defence mechanism –
the mucus bomb. As soon as the slug is attacked it secretes
so much mucus that the attacker loses its appetite!

"I have a real problem with slugs as there are three cats living next door
and two cats on the other side. Consequently in my postage stamp of
suburbia the birds do not come down to eat the slugs! The only thing
I can grow is tomatoes. Slugs don't like them."
Abi Mansley

Instruments of death

Is this a dagger I see before me – Macbeth

You have made worms' meat of me…a plague on both your houses
– Romeo and Juliet

If you prick us, do we not bleed? If you tickle us, do we not laugh?
If you poison us do we not die? And if you wrong us, shall we not revenge
– Merchant of Venice

If slugs eat their own kind why should we have any compulsion about squashing, burning, drowning, cutting, boiling or even freezing them? Because, as we said before, slugs do serve a purpose beyond the release of our own anger towards them. They are real life wombles… clearing up the things everyday folk leave behind.

"My father always carried a pocket knife which he referred to as his slug killer, or 'slugger' for short. Not a very efficient way of dealing with the problem but very satisfying."
Steve Rosser

"My normal method of slug killing is an old pair of scissors (known as the 'slug scissors') kept for the sole purpose of cutting slugs in half."
Jane Wheeler

"Scissors…My record is 1101 slugs in about an hour."
Ian Izett

"I take a hand fork and go out with a torch between 11pm
and midnight and spear them."
John Bolitho

"A sharp spade for giant slugs!"
Karen Leggett

"A good stamp with a Doc Martens boot will kill them."
Jane Wheeler

"I place a cirlce of bran around individual plants or rows of veg.
Slugs eat it and swell up – great food for the birds! It's available from
pet shops or in bulk from farm merchants (about £4 for a giant bag)."
Mrs W. Matthews

Though this be madness, yet there is method in it – Hamlet

"We use bran...it swells up inside them and they burst."
Beryl Swinton

"I have found that short of cutting them in half they are virtually indestructable. Best method is to seal them in a polythene bag so that they suffocate!"
Sally Starbuck

"I find Nemaslug is excellent for controlling slugs because it is so effective and easy to use."
Mrs P. Emery

"I would like to recommend Nemaslug as it does seem to have reduced the damage previously done by armies of small black slugs and the occasional monster. It has been particularly effective in the glasshouse."
Lynda Dolan

"Pour salt on the slugs and watch them fizzle to death."
Claire Johnson

My endeavours have ever come too short of my desires –
Henry VIII

"I have sprinkled salt all around the patio before their nightly constitutional and haven't seen a single slug or snail in two weeks. However, mysteriously, my sunflowers are completely chewed up and covered in slime. They must be absailing down the wall of the house!"
Joyce Pinto

Traps (that kill)

"After a boozy BBQ several empty beer cans were left strewn about the garden. When I collected them up the following morning nearly all had at least one slug inside. Because the cans were a self contained trap I could put them straight in the bin with none of the mess of a normal beer trap. However, I normally recycle all my cans and I'm not sure how keen the recycle centre would be on having slugs as well!"

Jane Wheeler

I do now remember the poor creature, small beer – Hamlet

"My best solution so far has been beer traps, but starting very early, in February and March. At this time there are no other interesting alternatives for the early slug to investigate, and so you catch and remove the slugs who will produce progeny, in their hundreds, thus saving plants later in the year."
Hilary Blyth

"I have eight slug pubs... I refill these when I remember and they are always full of dead and decomposing slugs. But the only way I am gaining any control over the numbers is to go out between 10.30 pm and midnight wearing a head torch and rubber gloves and pick them up... I do not use anything poisonous to birds / wildlife etc. as we encourage birds into the garden (we have thrushes) and as a veterinary nurse I have seen cats poisoned with metaldehyde."
Georgina M. Christian

"Place a container in the garden with milk in it. The slugs go in after the milk and cannot get out (like the beer trap), but using this method not only do you drown the slugs, but hedgehogs will drink the milk and eat the slugs; all you have to do is top up the milk."

Patrick Meads

"I have found Marmite jars to be excellent slug traps. There is enough yeast in a used jar to bait the trap; you need only to part bury the jar so the neck is clear of the ground surface (so beetles cannot fall in) and add a little water in the bottom. When the yeast is finished it works well with a little beer added to the water. I can catch several small slugs per night in one. The brown colour (of the jar) is unobtrusive in the garden."

John Cooper

Instruments of life

So you're still reading. Good. You've made it through to the
life-affirming part of the book.

They that have the power to hurt, and will do none;
they nightly do inherit Heaven's graces – Sonnet 94

In nature they do blemish but the mind; none can be called
deformed but the unkind – Twelfth Night

Traps (for picking off)

"I discovered a good way of catching slugs when the introduction of a third cat into our household made cat number two decide she would only eat outside. Uneaten cat food proved an incredible draw for slugs of all sizes if left out overnight...I put it in the middle of an opened-up newspaper at dusk and go out before I go to bed to collect whatever has turned up. Being somewhat soft-hearted, I tend to put the culprits either in the compost heap, where I hope they will do something useful, or if I'm at the far end of the garden I throw them over the other side of the stream, daring them to swim back! I think I've read that either slugs or snails will judge how plentifully to multiply by the amount of slime they find on the ground, thus avoiding the waste of producing young if there are enough adults already around for the amount of food available. This would seem to suggest that removing the offenders actually only opens the way for more to be bred, but I suppose there isn't much we can do about this."

Lyn Pullen

Barriers

"I found that copper rings with sifted cinders inside saved my hostas and lupins. We had to replace a copper hot water cylinder and so my husband cut it into strips about 2 inches wide, so that we had a number of circles of varying sizes (we could have them the full size of the original cylinder or fold the ends round each other to make the circle smaller). We have an anthracite fire so I was able to sift the cinders and fill the circles before the plants emerged in the spring. Incidentally, in winter the copper rings remind me where the plants are when they have gone to ground."

Greta F. Homewood

"Run a copper wire around the edge of your vegetable bed. Plug the ends into a potato or other vegetable. This creates an electromagnetic charge that slugs can't crawl across."
Claire Wade

"After learning that copper reacts with a slug's slime to give it an electric shock, I found a large length of copper tubing at a car boot sale and placed this on the earth, bending around the perimeter of my vegetable garden. So far, I have not yet had a leaf nibbled by a slug."
Sandra Seymour

"They definitely don't like electricity! I did try a wire laid on the ground connected to a 60v AC source but unfortunately it killed frogs as well."
Ian Izett

"Physically removing the slugs after it's rained (when they all come out) has helped the problem a bit. Also putting plant pots on a gravelled area seemed to discourage them (only works for potted plants though, obviously, but you could try building gravel barriers in beds?). A friend told me that a barrier of broken eggshells would work too, but unfortunately I don't eat enough eggs to try it out!"

Emma Snow

"I wash the eggshells out first, then place them on a metal tray which is stored in the oven. Take them out whilst the oven is on but put them back in the oven when you have switched it off; the residual heat will dry them and they will last longer. Then crush them with a rolling pin and sprinkle around your favourite plants."

Sue Catchpole

"I read that pine needles are acidic, and slugs being alkaline don't like acid, so after Christmas I retrieved the old Christmas tree before it got dumped and removed all the small branches and placed them round the hostas, lupins etc. This seemed to work until the needles turned brown."
Martyn Watts

"Seaweed draped around the plants (not too close to damage the crop) – they don't like the salt – has the added bonus of being an organic fertiliser."
Mrs Julie O'Day

"Take the fallen husks of the sweet chestnut and lay them around your plants in a dense mat. The slugs won't cross the prickly, brittle surface."
Beryl Greenaway

"Quite by accident we discovered a nearly foolproof method of slug deterrence – thanks to our compost. A mixture of old, used coffee grounds and broken-up eggshells and mussel shells spread around sensitive plants each spring works a treat; the caffeine deters them from feeding and the sharp (to them) edges of the egg and mussel shells keep them from approaching plants. Best of all, it helps fertilize the plants (works especially well for ericaceous plants) and is child / bird / animal friendly... All I know is that last year my hostas and delphiniums looked like swiss cheese and this year they are spotless!"
Alexandra Clarke

"I set seeds in toilet roll holders and when planting them out still in the holders I smear the tops of the holders with car grease mixed with salt."
Babs Payne

"In the greenhouse, a mini-moat around the legs of the staging excludes slugs and snails from climbing upwards. Large cottage cheese cartons, or similar, serve this purpose; fill them to the brim with water.
A very generous coating of Vaseline around the legs of staging serves the same purpose."
Mrs J. Cargill

"At the risk of tempting fate, my hostas are 100 per cent slug free since I began smearing Vaseline around the rims of their pots."
Nicola Noakes

"Baskets are placed 3' in the air and slugs don't seem interested in making the journey. Take a 4' post and knock it 1' into the ground. Screw a hanging basket to the top after removing the chains, then plant them up as usual. They are also great for people with bad backs or wheelchairs, and are perfect for trailing strawberries or herbs."

Brian Batty

"Use pieces of slabwood. These are simply artificial shelters for slugs that can be easily inspected. I have found the most effective traps to be lengths of slabwood obtained free from sawmills, i.e. the round-sided bits that are left behind after sawing a log. 'Proper' planks of wood are not so good because they tend to curl up in the hot sun and don't keep so damp underneath. The pieces of slabwood are placed between crop rows, where they provide handy mini-paths. You simply turn them up from time to time and remove the slugs. The only disadvantage of this method is that if you don't inspect the traps regularly, you are in fact helping the slugs by providing a very convenient shelter very close to the crops!"

Peter Harper, CAT

"I find sheep's fleece a wonderful way of deterring slugs."
R. L. Davies

"I have found a useful friend in defeating this eternal pest by using the dried leaves of *Berberis Darwinii* scattered around my beloved hostas."
Granville Stout

"Warm pee saturated around soil…"
Merlyn Peter

"I scatter wood and coal ash around my plants when the young shoots are coming up in spring, and find that the slugs leave them alone when treated in this way."
Mrs C. Kennedy

"Surround your plants (particularly vegetable plants) with woodchips or shavings or sawdust. About 1" thick, away from the stem of the plant. It's too dry and fibrous for slugs, so they find it difficult, or impossible, to reach the greenery. If it rains, sprinkle a fresh supply around the plants and ensure that they get sufficient water as the woodchips / shavings and / or sawdust are very absorbent. It's not 100 per cent foolproof, but is effective to a large degree."
Elaine White

"In springtime, slugs are particularly fond of wilted comfrey leaves. About a week after planting out, a pile of comfrey leaves is left in the centre of a plot. The slugs will soon find it and more and more will follow the slime trails. Don't do anything until about the fifth night when the pile is absolutely heaving with slugs. Remove these and dispose of them. On succeeding nights, further slugs can be removed but there will be far fewer. Finally, the pile of leaves is removed (and composted) and the plot is planted up with a continuous ring of comfrey leaves laid around the edge of the plot. After this, only occasional night-time checks are necessary, and renewal of the leaves every week or so."

Peter Harper, CAT

The nightly pick

Good night, good night! Parting is such sweet sorrow, that I shall say good night till it be morrow – Romeo and Juliet

Did my heart love till now? Forswear it sight! For I ne'er saw true beauty till this night – Romeo and Juliet

"People wonder who the hunched figure is prowling round the garden after 11pm brandishing a torch and a salt cellar belonging to the lady of the house! Well, no need to be fearful, it's only me on a slug hunt. Not so silly though – most nights I have a tally of 70 or 80. Some kind of liquid refreshment is required after that – blow this idea of giving it to the slugs! Guests thought I was a joke until they joined me –
now I'm not so daft."

Pat and Graham Moore

"Phew, I'm relieved to know that I'm not the only one who goes out lamping for slugs at night!!"
Martyn Watts

"Going out in the evening...and picking them up is as effective as anything."
Mrs S. Whateley

"I collect slugs and snails into a large yoghurt pot (with lid) while I am gardening and on 'hunts', usually first thing in the morning."
Miss Susanna Cooke

"My husband swears by 'slug watches' and every night we go out and pick off the slugs."
Emily Chapman

"I patrol each night after watering."
Katie Bailey

"I slug hunt after dark armed with a torch and a pair
of adapted old kitchen scissors."
Graham Hough

"I go out into the garden with a torch each evening and pick
up every slug and snail that I find."
Gordon Michie

And if you don't want to do it yourself – send the children out…

"I've tried lots of methods – but the only one that worked for me was the following recipe: ingredients – take a couple of competitive children; give incentive such as per slug treat or 1p per slug; send kids out to garden as evening falls (torches make it more fun); show them the obvious and not so obvious hiding places; leave them to collect as many as they can; give rewards."
Nicola Meneses

And if you can't beat them…

grow slug resistant plants

"I hate the b******s with a loathing beyond expression. There is NO WAY to beat them. I'm gradually moving to growing only plants that they don't eat, and giving up on growing annuals and anything tender."
Alison Carter

"We should, really, grow more plants they don't like."
Anne Davies

"Grow slug resistant plants. I discovered last year that they don't like busy-lizzies or begonias."
Howard Foster

"Plant lavender as a border to vegetable plots. Plant allium, garlic or wormwood near vulnerable plants. Use a few drops of essential oil of cedarwood or pine near vulnerable plants. Use fir cones as a barrier."
Anne Myers

"Plants that have not been eaten are blue ribbed hostas (variegated ones are very prone to slugs), geraniums, marjoram and sedum. Perhaps we should just plant these and stop worrying about the slugs and snails!"
Denise Keith

"I am about to give up the battle, frankly, and am considering regressing to a basic gardening principle: grow plants according to your conditions. If you have loads of slugs there's no point battling away to get rid of them all. Simply choose to grow plants that slugs don't eat."
Julian Ashworth

"In the end, I've had to give up planting their favourite plants, e.g. lettuce, and try alternatives such as spinach beet (freshly picked leaves are lovely in salad), although they still eat them a bit. In contrast, they haven't touched rocket, onions, garlic, chives, mint, sage, lavender, lemon balm, alpine strawberries and anything on established trees or bushes – so I'm sticking to those plants now!"
Emma Snow

Slug slime

"Is anyone working on an industrial application for this amazing substance? Can anyone recommend a good way of washing slug slime off fingers?"
Chris Madsen

"Re Chris Madsen and slug slime – keep hands dry after handling slugs, wipe off as much as possible with paper towels (which can then be composted), then wash off the rest."
Jenny Evans

The BBC's Robin Aitken reports that researchers have discovered unusual properties in the mucus secreted by giant African land snails, which they believe might have important applications in medical science. It could lead to a new treatment for broken bones. Head of research, Professor Viney has also studied mucus from slugs: "We've already established that slug slime, which many people would think of as a very simple, if messy substance, is in fact a complex material."

Slugs have other uses too…

"A dinghy was over-wintered, on its towing trailer, in a secluded corner of the garden. The bodywork became covered in a green algae and fallen leaves collected in the bottom. When we went to move the boat in the late spring we could see that the bows had been cleaned of algae and further investigation showed that a large colony of slugs and snails had taken up residence on the boat. During the day they hid amongst the leaves or under the edge of the boat and at night they came out and browsed the algae. It also solved the problem of what to do with the slugs we found in the rest of the garden – we throw them into the trailer as well."

Peter Wilson

The good

"I was so angry at the state of the flowers being eaten alive, I went on a slug rampage. Equipped only with a pair of Marigolds and a bucket, I upturned everything that might be sheltering a SLUG! I'd collected a good amount but decided (being a vegetarian) I couldn't bring myself to kill them, so I put them on the bird table. Watching them slowly slime off, I thought they're not getting the better of me! So I then poured salt all around the bird table, so they would have to stay and become bird food. I was horrified when they started to fizz, and realising what I'd done, quickly gathered them all back in the bucket and tried to rinse the salt off with the hosepipe! NEVER AGAIN! I throw them on the garden waste pile now. Frogs eat slugs don't they? By the way I'm getting married on March 30th to my boyfriend whose nickname is 'Slug'!"
Elva Davies

The ugly

A dish fit for the gods – Julius Caesar

"I am in the habit of swallowing large slugs whole. I don't particularly like the experience, but I must confess it doesn't bother me now as much as it did at first… Of course, if your readers baulk at the thought of consuming slugs they should seriously consider educating their children to perform said culinary cull. Children will willingly eat slugs with a little encouragement and, although I'm not sure, I hazard that said ubiquitous molluscs are a good deal more nutritious than the vast majority of prepackaged foods."

Peter Symons

Prevention is better than cure

Plants that slugs tend to avoid

As with anything to do with slugs there is disagreement about which plants are truly slug resistant. Slugs will have a go at just about anything if it's young enough and there isn't a tastier option. However, the opposite is also true. Most mature plants are somewhat slug resistant and a complete list would be encyclopedic.

Flowers

Foxgloves, fuschias, daisies, artemisias, alyssum, evening primrose,
lambs' ear, fox and cubs, most bulbs – snowdrops, fritillaries, geum,
wild garlic, alliums, daffodils, montbretia (crocosmia), rock rose,
honesty, schisostylis, lavatera, hollyhocks, azaleas, alyssum saxatile,
pelargonium, globe thistle, perennial geraniums, mallow, mullein,
holly, ivy, lungwort, hibiscus.

And what about hostas…

Hosta growers have told us that no hosta is immune but large
mature hostas and ones with upright leaves are best.

Decoy plants

Slugs are attracted to plants already contaminated by previous visitors. It's a good idea to have diversion plants next to those you want to protect, especially if they are seedlings. Yellow mustard is an excellent plant to use as bait. Cress or spinach plants also act as great decoys.

Dahlia, French marigold, tagetes and lupins are all slug favourites.

"Grow forget-me-nots around vulnerable plants. I usually spread seeds around willy nilly, then pull them up when flowering has finished."
Karen Leggett

Part Three

And if You Want to be Really Happy – what we do at CAT

If Britain is the capital of slugs, Wales must be the citadel of rain. Shakespeare said "for the rain it raineth every day", but for the people of Wales it isn't much better. The Centre for Alternative Technology is in the middle of Wales, near the ancient royal city of Machynlleth – famous for being the home of the Welsh prince, Owain Glyndŵr.

And if the rain wasn't enough to put us off horticulture we also chose to build our organic gardens on slate waste, which must be one of the most slug friendly materials known to man. Despite this, we don't have a terrible slug problem. This is what we do…

• Rotavate the vegetable plots every year at the start of the season. Not only does this kill a large amount of slugs, it brings slugs to the surface where the birds can feed off them.

• Improve the soil. We continually add compost to the soil to improve drainage and provide superior growing conditions for the plants. Slugs like heavy, wet soils, and weak plants.

- We rake and hoe regularly to destroy slug hiding places in the cracks of the soil and underneath weeds, and to disturb the slime trails and eggs (which look like little pearls) in the soil.

- We give our plants a good start in life. Growing them on raised beds in protected areas helps reduce slug damage. Using a good seed compost followed by a potting-on compost gives them strength. If we grow outside in a seed bed then we make sure it has been prepared to a high standard.

• Create habitats that encourage wildlife into the garden. We have created ponds and wildlife havens and have all the usual predators.

• Pick nightly if we need to and dispose of slugs away from the critical areas. Quite often they go into the compost heap. We adopt a humane approach to the removal process. It is not necessary to salt, burn or otherwise kill them. Our gardener Roger McLennan will not kill slugs.

• Only then do we start to use barriers, traps and tools
– and most of the time we don't need to.

Part Four

And the winner is…

Barriers

– woodchip/sawdust, ash, the shells of brazils, walnuts, pistachios, sweet chestnut and/or eggs, slate/gravel chips, recycled glass chippings, pine cones, sand, sheeps' fleece, cocoa shell and other mulches – 15 per cent.

Nightly picking

and disposal by drowning in salty or boiling water, drowning in the toilet, freezing, burning, salting, or for the more compassionate: the gentle and surreptitious sport of neighbour's-fence pitch-and-toss; to the tip via the wheelie bin, or direct to wasteland – 13.4 per cent.

Beer traps

(mostly homemade from yoghurt pots, Rachel's Dairy Organic being one suggestion, margarine tubs, Marmite jars, or bought) – 10 per cent.

And the runners up...

Salt or salty water – 9 per cent.
Birds/toads/hedgehogs – 5.6 per cent.
Rub Vaseline or Marmite, yeast extract or grease
on stems or around pots – 5.6 per cent.
Bantam chickens/Indian Runner ducks – 5.5 per cent.
Scissors (for the snip) and knives – 4.5 per cent.
Nemaslug – 3.9 per cent.
Copper rings/wire – 3.9 per cent.
Grow decoy plants/weeds
(comfrey is a particular favourite) – 3.9 per cent.
Let them eat bran – 2.8 per cent.
Grow plants inedible to slugs – 2.2 per cent.
Collect under paving slabs/plank – 1.7 per cent.
Build a moat around your plants
(sometimes called a batcombe box) – 1.2 per cent.

Grapefruit skins – 1.2 per cent.
Send the children out – 1.2 per cent.
Put milk, or soya milk in a saucer; they seem to like it – 1.2 per cent.
Electric fence – 0.6 per cent.
Badgers – 0.6 per cent.
Raise plants above the ground (on stilts if necessary) – 0.6 per cent.
Plant more than you need – 0.6 per cent.
Keep your beds clean and hoe regularly – 0.6 per cent.
Feed cat/dog food and pick them off – 0.6 per cent.
Protect with plastic bottles – 0.6 per cent.
Blast them with infrared! – 0.6 per cent.
Eat them
(but swallow them whole as they don't taste very nice) – 0.6 per cent.

Acknowledgements

The Little Book of Slugs has many authors. The contributors to the Bug-the-Slug campaign, those included in the book and those we did not have room to include; Chloe Ward and Peter Harper, who helped to compile the lists of slug resistant plants, and make our Bug-the-Slug garden at BBC Gardeners' World Live, the rest of the BBC Gardeners' World Live team, and the numerous CAT staff who have contributed ideas to our campaign and to the formulation of this book. In particular we would like to thank CAT gardeners Roger McLennan and Eryl Davies, and also Caroline Oakley, Graham Preston, Martin Donnelly and the CAT Mail Order crew for their continued enthusiasm.

Sources and resources

Les limaces sous contrôle,
Claudia Graber and Henri Suter, Terre Vivante, 1991
The Organic Way, HDRA, 2002
Common Garden Remedies – A Gardening Guide,
Janet Thomson, July 2000
Pesticide Poisoning of Animals 2000:
Investigations of Suspected Incidents in the United Kingdom –
Wildlife Incidents Investigation Scheme. Full
report available from www.defra.gov.uk
Veterinary Poisons Information Service (VPIS) in London offers services
to vets on subscription but does not answer general enquiries
www.pan-uk.org/pestnews/homepest/slugs.htm website of the
Petsicides Action Network

www.cf.ac.uk/biosi/research/biodiversity/staff/wocs2.html
This is the website of Dr Bill Symondson, invertebrate ecologist,
and includes details of the safe use of slug pellets and alternatives.
www.themolluscicide.com or www.metaldehyde.com
for the manufacturers' angle on slug pellets.
www.letsgogardening.co.uk/information/connect2/slugpellets.htm
has the manufacturers' press release in full.
http://drzeus.best.vwh.net/Slugs.html
for a picture of slugs in love!
www.maths.gla.ac.uk/~mab/Biocontrol/Slugs.html
for general information.

Has anyone seen where my lettuce has gone?

Not so long ago in the warm wet days of spring
I planted out a happy, healthy marigold seedling
I nurtured it for days and I thought t'would be all right
but a slimy slug has come along and scoffed it all last night!

They've avoided all my radishes but gobbled up m' cabbages
Has anyone seen where my lettuce has gone?
My beans are decimated, I'm just so devastated
I thought I was a gardener – oh where have I gone wrong?

I cannot let them have it all, I'm damned if I will share
I've tried everything from egg shells to sweepings of barber's hair
I yearn to pop 'em in a pot and cover 'em in salt
Watch them sizzle in a tizzle, (oh it's such a lovely thought!)

I dream of squashing and a-squishing till my veggie beds are clear
If only Roger'd let me drown them in a pint of organic beer
'What a waste of lovely ale!' (and what comes next I always fear)
'I'm afraid you'll have to HOE! Put your back into it, my dear!'

So at the start of veggie season we've been out in rain or shine
To hoe around the plants and eradicate slug slime
The eggs come to the surface, they dry out and will not hatch
'Cos they're mostly made of water (and the rest's my cabbage patch!)

'We can't squash 'em – don't you kill 'em!!' We've all heard Roger cry,
'Or you may be held to ransom by that great slug in the sky.'

Susanna 'Ted' Waters – CAT's slug warrior 2002

ihateslugs.com

• Order anti-slug products from The Slug Trap –
our on-line mail order service

• Join Bug-the-Slug and contribute to the next edition of
The Little Book of Slugs

• Find out the facts about slug pellet poisoning

• From here visit our other websites
www.cat.org.uk and
www.ecobooks.co.uk
and buy a wide range of green books and products

Special Offer

❏ I would like to find out more about CAT and claim my 10 per cent discount voucher to spend on my first purchase of slug products from CAT's mail order service – *Buy Green By Mail*

Please send me…

❏ CAT's Slug Trap mail order product list.

❏ A list of CAT's leisure and professional development courses, including organic gardening (as featured on BBC Holiday Programme).

❏ CAT's mail order catalogue with hundreds of green books and products, and details of our unique green wedding list service.

❏ A membership form. I am interested in joining CAT (annual membership £16.00) and taking advantage of CAT's five special membership benefits.

❏ A publications list, including details of Pippa Greenwood recommended *Creative Sustainable Gardening* and 80 other titles for the home and garden.

Name _____

Address _____

_____

_____

Telephone _____

email _____

No further mailings from CAT please ☐

Please send to Allan Shepherd, CAT, Machynlleth, Powys, Wales SY20 9AZ.